LIFE DURING THE GREAT CIVILIZATIONS

The Ottoman Empire

Lucile Davis

BLACKBIRCH®
PRESS

THOMSON
™
GALE

San Diego • Detroit • New York • San Francisco • Cleveland • New Haven, Conn. • Waterville, Maine • London • Munich

LIBRARY OF CONGRESS CATALOGING-IN-PUBLICATION DATA

Davis, Lucille.
  The Ottoman Empire / by Lucille Davis.
      p. cm. — (Life during the great civilizations)
Includes bibliographical references and index.
Contents: Islam guided the government — Families, their homes and clothing — Working and relaxing — Enduring art and architecture of the Ottomans.
  ISBN 1-56711-739-2 (alk. paper)
  1. Turkey—Civilization—Juvenile literature. 2. Turkey—Social life and customs—Juvenile literature. 3. Art, Turkish—Juvenile literature. 4. Architecture, Turkish—Juvenile literature. 5. Islam and state—Turkey—History. [1. Turkey—Civilization. 2. Turkey—History—Ottoman Empire, 1288-1918. 3. Turkey—Social life and customs.] I. Title. II. Series.

  DR432.D385 2003
  956.1'015—dc22   2003015299

Printed in United States
10 9 8 7 6 5 4 3 2 1

Content

Last of the Ancient Empires

The Ottoman Empire has been called the last of the ancient empires. From the fourteenth to the sixteenth centuries, it was the geographic center of the civilized world. Three major continents—Europe, Asia, and Africa—surrounded it and many land trade routes between these continents went through the Ottoman Empire. Trade caravans that passed through paid tariffs on the goods they carried.

The people who established the empire were nomadic Turks, who came out of the plains of northeastern Europe on the border with China and Mongolia. Excellent horsemen and warriors, they learned how to be good administrators from the Greeks. Their travels brought them in contact with Arabs, who introduced them to the religion of Islam. The wandering Turkish tribes settled in what today is known as Turkey.

A man named Osman (pronounced Othman in Arabic) united the Turkish tribes of Asia Minor in 1299 and began to build an empire

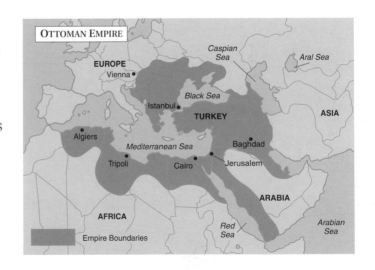

Opposite Page: Mehmed II conquered all of Asia Minor and Eastern Europe, and made them part of the Ottoman Empire.

After Mehmed II captured Constantinople (pictured) in 1453, he renamed it Istanbul and made it the capital of the Ottoman Empire.

that carried his name (Ottoman is the Westernized version of Othman). Osman, a convert to Islam, created a government based on the religion's holy book, the Koran. When his son, Orhan, became ruler, he adopted the title of sultan.

The armies of the Ottoman sultan expanded the borders of the empire throughout Asia Minor and Eastern Europe. Mehmed II, "the Conqueror," brought all of Asia Minor and the Balkans under Ottoman control. He captured Constantinople, the capital of the Byzantine Empire, in 1453. The city was renamed Istanbul and became the capital of the Ottoman Empire. Under Mehmed the lands of the empire stretched from Budapest on the Danube to Aswan on the Nile, and from the Euphrates River almost to Gibraltar. Ottoman civilization under Mehmed's son, Süleyman the Magnificent, was open and mobile. Süleyman allowed peoples brought under the banner of the empire to retain their own religion and culture. All he required of them was to pay taxes and not revolt against the empire.

Süleyman reigned from 1520 to 1566, a period some historians consider the golden age of the Ottoman Empire. Süleyman was a contemporary of Christopher Columbus, whose voyages opened the Americas to exploration and eventual trade. By the time Süleyman died, the Ottoman Empire was no longer at the center of world trade. Although the empire ended with the ouster of Sultan Mehmed VI and the establishment of the Republic of Turkey in 1923, its importance as a historical link between East and West endures.

CHAPTER ONE

Islam Guided the Government

An Ottoman sultan's power over his empire was absolute. His political decisions, however, had to be guided by Islam.

The Ottoman Turks were Muslims, which means they were followers of Islam. To become a Muslim requires only a profession of faith: "I testify that there is no god but Allah; Muhammad is the Prophet of Allah." To continue in the faith requires four additional practices: pray five times a day, give to the poor, fast during the holy month of Ramadan, and if possible, make a pilgrimage to the holy city of Mecca. The five daily prayers can be observed anywhere except those on Fridays at noon, when prayer in a congregation at a mosque, a Muslim building of worship, is required. Friday services at the mosque begin when the muezzin, a mosque official, calls the faithful to pray. The imam, chief religious official of the mosque, leads the service. In a large mosque other religious leaders help the imam conduct Friday prayers. At smaller mosques, one person leads the service.

Any man can become an imam or prayer leader. Islam has no ranks of clergy to rule over the faithful, because, according to the teachings of Muhammad, no man can come between Allah and a worshiper. Muslims are guided by the Koran and a collection of traditions known as the hadith. The sacred book of Islam is the Koran, and Muslims believe it is the word of Allah, or God, revealed to his prophet Muhammad. The hadith is believed to be Muhammad's point of view on a wide range of issues.

Opposite Page: The Turks of the Ottoman Empire were Muslims. Every Friday at noon, they gathered at mosques, like the mosque of Süleyman the Magnificent (pictured), to pray.

The principles of Islamic law were the foundation of the Ottoman Empire's legal system. Although sultans wrote laws called kanuns, *they always deferred to the sacred law of Islam.*

The Koran and the hadith are the basis of Islamic law. Together they are known as sharia. By studying sharia, religious leaders can give advice in five categories—forbidden, disapproved, permitted, recommended, and obligatory. This was the basis of the empire's legal system.

The Legal System

Muslims were in charge of the empire's legal system, which operated under the direction of the ulema, the leaders of law and religion. These leaders included mosque officials, religious teachers, *qadis* and muftis. *Qadis* judges—and muftis advisers—administered the law. Their services were paid for out of religious donations. Additional funding came from fees and fines paid after a legal question was decided. A special department of the Ottoman treasury handled the money.

A *qadi* was appointed to each district. The *qadi* sat as judge for the district and appointed deputies to help him. He also acted as local registrar and officiated at weddings. A *qadi* and mufti were appointed to serve large cities. A mufti advised the *qadi* on legal matters. Government administrators often consulted with *qadi*, as well as muftis, on legal matters related to the operation of the government.

When a legal issue came before a *qadi*, he had three sets of laws to consult. Sharia stood as law over everyone, including the sultan, and covered all issues of life including religious, legal, social, ethical, and economic matters. In addition, *qadi* consulted the *kanuns* and the *adet* to help them decide legal issues. The *kanuns* were the written decrees of the sultans. The *adet* detailed local customs. Sacred law, however, always took precedence over the sultans' law and local custom.

If a *qadi* could not find an answer to a legal question before him, he turned to a mufti for advice. The mufti would restate the question using fictional names to represent the people involved in the case. By restating the case in general terms and using fictional names, the mufti was able to find a similar case within sharia. When a mufti reached a decision, he issued an answer, called a *fetva*. The answer could be a simple "yes" or "no," or it could be a more detailed answer backed by scripture from the Koran. Whether the question before him addressed a religious or civil matter, the mufti's answer was final.

Government: A Military Administration

The Ottoman Empire's government was organized as a military administration. District governors were appointed from the ranks of military officers. Ottoman sultans gave land to Muslim men in exchange for military service. These landholders became officers. Since the officers acquired their land and wealth by serving the sultan, this made the officers who administered the districts very loyal to the Ottoman ruler.

The officers who governed the various districts of the Ottoman Empire were loyal to the sultan since he often gave them land and wealth to reward their service.

Slaves taken during battles of conquest were turned over to the sultan to be trained as soldiers. When the supply of slaves dwindled, the sultan required non-Muslim families to give him a male child, aged ten to twenty, as a slave, a practice called *devshirme*. The boys were educated and trained for the Janissary Corps, the company of slave soldiers. Those chosen for the Janissary Corps could obtain both high position and wealth, but these things could not be passed along. According to Baron Wratislaw, a Bohemian nobleman who visited the court of Süleyman the Magnificent: "On their death, the Emperor will say: 'Thou hast been my man, thou hast gained wealth from me; it is a proper thing that after thy death it should be returned back . . . to me.'" [1]

Devshirme

Some boys who were chosen in the devshirme, *a system of collecting young boys for future military service, served the sultan in his palace.*

The *devshirme*, the collecting of young boys, provided the Ottoman sultans with well-trained administrators and soldiers. The boys were selected on the basis of looks, good physical condition, and moral standards.

They were converted to Islam, educated, and trained in a trade or craft. They were fed, clothed, and strictly disciplined, with a particular emphasis on obedience and good manners. During their period of education, they acted as palace pages. They were schooled in poetry, literature, history, law, and religion, and were taught to read and write in three languages: Turkish, Arabic, and Persian. Turkish was the language of the courts, the Koran was written in Arabic, and Persian was the language of poetry and literature.

A leader of the Janissary Corps, like the one pictured here, could attain great wealth. Upon his death, however, all of his belongings would belong to the sultan once more.

Boys taken in the *devshirme* could also be selected for palace service and were trained to become government administrators and appointed governors of towns and provinces to replace the military appointees. If they proved themselves good at this work, they were promoted and sent back to the sultan's palace to help run the empire. It was even possible for one of these boys to rise to the position of grand vizier, the sultan's personal adviser. Those who became administrators obtained great power and wealth. Those taken in the *devshirme* were slaves of the sultan and could not pass on their wealth.

Since military officers owed their wealth and the slave soldiers owed their lives to the sultan, they were very loyal to him. This enabled Ottoman sultans to rule and keep watch, through their loyal administrators, over their vast empire. With sharia as the law of the empire, the sultan was able to leave the administration of the legal system in the hands of the Muslim clerics. In addition, the sultans were wise enough to be flexible when it came to ruling over non-Muslim peoples, who were allowed to follow their own religious laws. The Sultans merely required non-Muslim people to remain loyal and pay taxes to the empire.

CHAPTER TWO

Families, Homes, and Clothing

Ottoman government levied taxes by the *hane* (household), which consisted of a married man with an independent income and his wife and children. To the government, a *hane* represented an economic unit. In a rich family, only the male head of the household worked to support his family. In poorer households, all the members worked. This was particularly true for farm families since even the women of the family helped plant and harvest crops. Usually no more than two generations lived in a household. An adult son might live at home while he learned his father's trade, but if that son were married and had an independent income, the government counted the son and his wife as a separate *hane*.

Daily Life

Daily life in the Ottoman Empire did not march to the ticking of a clock. Ogier Ghiselin de Busbecq, diplomat of the Holy Roman Empire to the Ottoman sultan's court in the mid–sixteenth century, wrote to a friend about this: "The (Ottoman) Turks have no hours to mark the time, just as they have no milestones to mark distances."[2]

Instead, the calls to prayer marked the time of day. Families rich and poor rose at dawn to the chant of a muezzin. Each family member washed before prayers. When all were dressed and gathered in one place, the men of the family knelt on rugs placed so they prayed facing Mecca, Islam's holy city. The females of the family, who were not allowed to

Opposite Page: Women of the Ottoman Empire lived together in harems, which sheltered and protected them from men who were not related to them.

Muslim men knelt on prayer rugs that faced the holy city of Mecca when they prayed. The five daily calls to prayer divided each day.

pray, knelt at the back of the room and listened behind a screen away from the men. After dawn prayers, the day began. The men of the family went to work and boys over the age of five went to school. Just after noon, the men stopped to pray on a prayer rug each kept at work or carried with him. After prayers, the men ate a meal and then returned to work. Halfway between noon and nightfall, the call to prayer came again so men stopped working and repeated the prayer ritual. After sundown, family members gathered at home for evening prayers, which were followed by dinner. The day ended with the family gathered once again for prayers before they slept.

A Father's Life

A father held absolute power over those who lived under his care. He was his family's source of income and was responsible for their religious life. He also chose mates for his unmarried children and other unmarried females such as a sister, aunt, or cousin in his care. The peasant-class father had the additional duty of doing the shopping for the family. A rich man had slaves for that purpose. Whether rich or poor, a married woman was not allowed to be seen in such a public place as an open bazaar.

A Mother's Life

A mother's life was restricted to her home. All women in the family lived in a harem. This word came from two Arabic words, *harim*, meaning "something forbidden" and *haram*, meaning "sanctuary."

Unless a woman was around only her husband or close relatives, she had to wear a veil that covered her face.

The harem kept a woman sheltered from men who were not her relatives. Within her home, however, a mother ruled over the women of the household. She directed the lives of all her children including any of her sons, married or unmarried, who still lived at home. Although the father gave the final approval for his children's marriage, it was the mother who did the matchmaking.

What People Wore

Articles of dress were similar for women and men. The basic outfit consisted of full trousers tied at the ankles, a loose-fitting shirt/smock, a short jacket or vest, and a caftan or long gown tied with a sash.

Rich men had slaves who shopped for the family since married women were not allowed to go to bazaars or other such public places.

Except for the quality of cloth, the outfit was the same for rich and poor.

Wealthy women owned more elaborate clothing. To the basic outfit, a wealthy woman added a fitted vest over her embroidered smock. Over this was added an ankle-length caftan of silk or wool tied with a sash. In cold weather a brocade robe, leather boots, and a tasseled cap completed the outfit. Women were required to wear veils before anyone except their husbands and close relatives.

Men wore the same basic outfit with a few differences. A sash was tied around the shirt, which created a kind of pocket where money, tobacco, and anything else they needed might be carried. A length of cloth wrapped

around a felt cap created a turban headdress. Wealthy men wore caftans of brocade pulled over trousers, shirt, and jacket. Heavy yellow leather shoes, pulled over leather socks, were worn outdoors. Loose-fitting, thick black boots were worn for riding.

Over time, clothing color and style became very important, as it marked an individual's place in society. Mehmed the Conqueror enacted sumptuary laws to help bring order to the empire. Sumptuary laws ban extravagant spending on moral or religious grounds. This limited what could be spent on clothing. Since wealth and position could not be displayed through a large wardrobe, people adopted specific styles of dressing to indicate their position in society. For example, wealthy Turkish men wore red trousers and yellow slippers. Dustmen, who provided cleaning services, wore red leather smocks. Holy men wound turban cloths around skullcaps to create a flatter, wider headdress. Armenians wore violet slippers and purple trousers, which separated them from Greeks, who wore black slippers and trousers. Clothing style as a mark of status and position became so important that Sultan Süleyman the Magnificent instituted a long list of regulations that governed what people could and should wear. These strict clothing laws established the Ottoman Empire style for the next 150 years. Before the laws were enacted, people in the empire had the opportunity to improve their social status. After clothing style and color became mandated by law,

Wealthy members of Ottoman society lived in large homes with many rooms. Rugs, pillows, and divans that could be moved easily furnished the multipurpose rooms.

Rooms with No Corners

The Ottomans disliked hard lines and sharp angles. According to folklore, impish jinni, or genies, hid in dark corners, so corners were to be avoided. Low sofas or cupboards were built into the angles of a room. Some corners were filled with an array of rugs and pillows. Sometimes a doorway was placed at the juncture of two walls to avoid having the two walls come together in a corner.

Because the Ottomans thought genies hid in dark corners, they often disguised the angles of a room with sofas, rugs, and pillows.

social mobility stopped because anyone found to be wearing an outfit not covered by the sumptuary regulations could be arrested.

Ottoman Homes

No matter their social status, Ottoman families lived in individual units. They did not live in apartments or share a house with another family.

Poor families lived in one-room dwellings. Floors were packed earth that was sometimes covered with reed mats. Peasant families had little or no furniture. The rugs and mattresses they used as beds were rolled up and stored against a wall during the day. In one area of the room a small collection of pots and spoons stood next to a cookstove. In one corner of the dwelling, a sink or large bowl was kept for washing.

Homes for the wealthy had many rooms. Even the wealthy, however, had little formal furniture. They used carpets, rugs, cushions, and divans to furnish their rooms, which were intended for general use rather than being designated as bedroom, living room, or dining room. Sir Charles Eliot, traveling in the empire, described the general-use room this way: "You sit in a room . . . when you are hungry you call; a little table is brought in and you eat; when you want to go to bed, a pile of rugs is laid . . . and you go to sleep."[3]

Though the rooms in their homes might not be strictly ordered, the rest of Ottoman citizens' lives were. The call to prayer ordered their daily lives, the laws of Islam governed them, the mandates of the sultan set dress codes and taxes, and guilds regulated their work.

CHAPTER THREE

Work and Relaxation

Work in the Ottoman Empire was not only thought to be necessary, it was considered an honorable duty. Few wealthy men devoted themselves to lives of leisure. Most of them worked as senior administrators for the government and managed their own estates. Even sultans were required to learn a skill or craft. Mehmed the Conqueror was a master gardener; Süleyman the Magnificent was a goldsmith. The rulers' participation in these activities testified to the nobility of work. It also showed solidarity with the trade guilds that controlled every type of work.

Work Guilds

Guilds controlled work in the empire. A guild was an organization of people who did the same kind of work. Guild regulations covered the place, clothing, and tools of work for guild members. Every trade, business, and profession operated under a guild concession, which was permission to operate a business. A monopoly is complete control over an area of work by one individual or business. Guilds granted warrants, or guarantees, to individuals to do business or practice their trade in a given area for a fixed amount of time. When business for that area was good, more warrants were granted. If business dropped off, warrants were allowed to lapse and no new ones were issued. Business practices and trade skills were set by the guilds. Fines and even

Opposite Page: All tradesmen and craftsmen belonged to guilds, organizations that rigidly controlled all aspects of work in the empire.

Merchants who did not comply with guild regulations were fined or even imprisoned.

prison sentences were levied to any guild member who did not comply with guild regulations.

Guilds contained masters, journeymen, and apprentices organized under a guild leader who carried the title of "sheikh." A steward managed guild money and a disciplinary officer handed out fines and punishments to uphold guild regulations and honor.

In exchange for submission to the rigid control of the guilds, individual members were guaranteed work. In hard times, the guild supported them with food and expense money. Members could also receive loans at low rates to expand their business or rebuild after a fire or other accident.

Every ten to twenty years, a guild would organize a festival to celebrate and showcase its members' work. Since most guilds were headquartered in large cities, the festival was a good excuse for a picnic in

Guild Apprenticeship

A young man who wanted to learn a trade apprenticed himself to a guild master. The master would teach the apprentice the skills of the trade and the secrets and traditions of the guild. It took years of training before an apprentice could be considered for guild membership initiation. When an apprentice appeared ready for initiation, his father would petition the sheikh to rule on whether the apprentice was ready. If the sheikh agreed, an initiation ceremony date was set, and the apprentice presented examples of his work to be judged by a council of craftsmen. If the pieces passed judgment, they were displayed at the initiation ceremony. At the end of the ceremony, the new member was presented to the guild. The displayed craft pieces were auctioned and the money presented to the new member as capital to set up his own shop. A party followed the initiation.

the country. It was a combination of social event and trade fair where individuals set up booths to demonstrate and display their work.

Evliya Celebi, a traveler in the empire, watched a parade of guilds in Istanbul that was ordered by the sultan. Every guild in the city passed by him as they demonstrated the skills of their trade, craft, or business. Celebi called the demonstrations of skill "tricks" when he wrote about the parade this way: "All these guilds pass in waggons or on foot, with the instruments of their handicraft, and are busy with great noise at their work. . . . These guilds pass (by) . . . with a thousand tricks . . . followed by their sheikhs."[4]

This painting depicts one of the guild festivals that were held every few years to demonstrate the skills and crafts of the members of the guild.

Relaxation

The biggest festival in the empire came at the end of Ramadan, the sacred month of fasting. The high point of Ramadan is the Night of Power, the twenty-seventh day of the ninth month, which celebrates Allah's revelation of the Koran to Muhammad. Two days later the holy month was over, and the festival began. Street vendors and entertainers such as musicians, acrobats, and storytellers appeared. A popular entertainment at this festival was the Karagöz, a shadow puppet theater. The puppets were jointed and mounted on sticks. One man moved the puppets and told the story using various voices and vocal noises. The plot of the story was carried by two main characters: Karagöz, a resourceful man of the

street; and Hajivat, who represented the educated man who thought too much of himself. The stories were usually funny and included events of local interest. The tales were satirical and the jokes were a bit crude. The story would be cleaned up for presentation in homes where women and children could see the show. Most often, though, the show found its audience in the coffee shops.

Coffeehouses

Men gathered in coffee shops to smoke, drink coffee, and amuse themselves. Musicians and entertainers often added to the atmosphere of the coffeehouses. It was a natural setting for the off-color humor of the Karagöz puppet shows. In addition, jugglers, magicians, and storytellers entertained the men. Women were not allowed in these places, but now and then dancing boys would entertain in the coffeehouses. The wives and daughters of Ottoman men, however, could not be seen out in public.

Bathhouses

Women were rarely allowed to participate in public events or festivities, but they could go to hammams, or public bathhouses. The visit to

Karagöz Puppet Shows

Karagöz puppet shows were performed on a raised platform in a three-sided booth. A wood shelf stood across the opening. A cotton screen, about three by four feet, was strung across the front of the booth above the

Karagöz puppet shows were popular coffeehouse entertainment.

shelf. An oil lamp sat under the shelf. At performance time, the puppet master lit the lamp and a three-man musical group struck up a tune that signaled the beginning of the play. The puppets were raised behind the lamp, which projected shadows on the cotton screen.

The puppets, which were about fifteen inches high, were made out of camel skin and painted in bright colors. The figures were then oiled to make them translucent. When raised behind the lamp, the puppets created colored shadows behind the screen.

a hammam was a daylong event attended by all the females of a household. Women and girls washed, visited with friends, and enjoyed food and gossip during their stay. The bathhouse was a place a prospective bride might be seen and questioned by the prospective groom's mother for suitability. It was also a place never visited by males of any age. There were separate public bathhouses for men.

The bathhouses held no bathtubs. The Ottoman people held a strong dislike of still water, which they believed could be a hiding place for mischievous jinni, or genies. Instead of bathtubs, copper spouts poured hot water into marble basins. Bathers, who wore wooden platform shoes to keep from slipping on marble floors, filled brass bowls with water and poured it over their bodies. Artists created beautiful tile patterns on the floors and intricately carved wall designs around the waterspouts to make the surroundings pleasing for the women. The decorations and attentive bath assistants helped make the trip to a hammam a much anticipated event.

The most anticipated event of the year, however, was the holy month of Ramadan when much preparation was required of both men and women. Rich or poor, every Muslim family participated as their circumstances allowed. Some wealthy Muslims hired orators and entertainers to perform in their courtyards, which they opened to the public.

CHAPTER FOUR

Enduring Art and Architecture of the Ottomans

The best artists, entertainers, and scholars could be found in Istanbul, called to the Ottoman capital by Süleyman the Magnificent. Many historians believe he reigned over a golden age when the empire was at the height of power and influence. Under this sultan, Ottoman art and architecture influenced artists throughout Europe and the Middle East.

Architecture

One of the artists Süleyman summoned to Istanbul was Mimar Sinan, a military builder, whom many consider the greatest of the Ottoman architects. Sinan's career lasted fifty years and his style influenced mosque architecture for centuries.

Sinan built hundreds of buildings during his lifetime. In addition to his military projects, he created civil buildings such as almshouses, baths, villas, granaries, fountains, aqueducts, hospitals, and caravanseries, lodgings for caravans of traders and merchants. His religious buildings included chapels, tombs, schools, mosques, and madrassas, or religious schools. It was his mosque designs that brought him recognition as one of the most famous producers of classic Ottoman architecture.

Sinan took his design inspiration from Saint Sophia Church, which had been built in what was then Constantinople. He wanted to create a large space under a domed roof with natural lighting from windows. Before Sinan, architects had built mosques in

Opposite Page: Ottoman architect Mimar Sinan considered the Selimiye Mosque (pictured) his masterpiece.

Sinan designed the Selimiye Mosque to have a large, bright interior space under a series of half domes and arches.

sections using half domes supported by thick walls placed around an open court. This style left the interiors small and dark. Sinan wanted to bring all the sections together under one dome. To do this, he developed a series of interior half domes and arches supported by huge piers and designed to create a large interior space lit by rows of windows under the arches. Art historians and Sinan, himself, consider the Selimiye Mosque at Edirne his masterwork. Here the one-time barracks builder achieved all he planned by bringing all the elements of the building under one large dome.

Although Sinan was and is honored as an outstanding architect, he did not think of himself that way. He considered himself a master craftsman. Speaking about his work, he said: "Shehzade mosque was my apprenticeship, the Suleymaniye my journeyman's work, the Selimiye at Edirne my masterpiece."[5]

Before Sinan achieved his domed design, mosques offered only small dark compartments in which to pray. Sinan's design brought the Muslim congregation together in a large, sunlit space for religious services. With sunlight bathing the floors and walls of the mosque, the tile work of the building gained greater importance.

Tile Work

Tile work used in the creation of Sinan's mosques became an integrated part of the interior design. Tiles of various colors and shapes were

Sinan, the Architect

This statue of Mimar Sinan, erected at his birthplace in Anatolia, honors the man many consider the greatest architect of the Ottoman Empire.

Mimar Koca Sinan was born to Greek Christian parents in Anatolia in 1489. Taken in a *devshirme,* he became a soldier. He advanced quickly from cavalry officer to construction officer and began to build bridges, barracks, and military towers. His advancement continued when his reputation as an accomplished builder and architect reached the attention of the sultan. In 1538, Süleyman appointed him "architect of the abode of felicity," or chief architect to the royal house.

laid on floors to create geometric designs, which helped accentuate the open worship space under the dome. Walls were decorated with tiled panels depicting objects from nature. Süleyman's summons brought artists from many parts of the world, who added design elements to tile art from as far away as China. These artists created their designs and sent them to the pottery in Iznik south of Istanbul.

Iznik was the most important pottery center during the late fifteenth and early sixteenth centuries. The *cuerda seca* method of glazing, which enabled artists to create more detailed and complex designs, was developed at Iznik.

Turkish Rugs

Rugs were an important part of life for people of the Ottoman Empire. Rugs covered floors and walls of most homes, each Muslim man owned at least one prayer rug, and rugs were an essential part of mosque furnishings. Rug making, already established as a high art form, advanced in the Ottoman Empire as more territory was added. New colors and weaving techniques came from Azerbaijan and Egypt. Persia introduced a red vegetable dye that gave Turkish carpets a distinct background color. It was the combination of the Persian knot and

Cuerda Seca Glazing

The cuerda seca *method of glazing allowed tile artists to create even more detailed designs.*

A red paste was spread over tiles and coated with white slip, which is watery clay. A design was stamped or carved into the surface of the tiles, then color glazes were applied. The design was outlined in a mixture of beeswax or vegetable fat and manganese oxide, a naturally occurring metallic element used to color bricks and ceramics. Firing melted away the wax or fat and left a red or black outline around the design. This also prevented the different colors of glaze from running together.

Egyptian wool that enabled Ottoman carpet weavers to achieve a high place in carpet art.

To make a carpet, an artisan wove a backing, then painted a design on it before the pile, the raised strands of yarn that form the surface of the carpet, was knotted onto the backing. The Persian knot combined with the silky Egyptian wool brought the ends of the pile closer together, creating a velvety surface.

Some of the finest examples of Turkish carpet making were produced during Süleyman's reign. So fine were these carpets, a tiny mistake was worked into each piece to avoid the consequences of the evil eye or envious jinni. It was thought that either could cause harm to or destroy a perfect carpet.

Although the Ottoman people retained their superstitions about the jinni, their lives were ordered by the call to prayer and sometimes moved to the beat of military drums. In fact, military drum corps or bands often played outside mosques following mid-afternoon prayers.

As the art form of making Turkish rugs reached new heights during the Ottoman Empire, artisans began to weave a tiny mistake into each piece to avoid the wrath of jealous genies.

Army Bands

Mehters, or army bands, often played after prayer services at mosques in large cities. Bands were assigned to certain government

officials, and the size of the band was determined by the official's rank. For example, the palace band included ninety musicians, and the grand vizier had forty-five musicians at his disposal. Instruments for the bands included fifes, drums, cymbals, and tambourines.

Percussion instruments were very important to Turkish musical groups. A percussion section could be quite large and include many different sizes of drums, cymbals, tambourines, and other rhythmic noisemakers. Europeans first heard the *mehters* of the Turkish army sometime in the early sixteenth century and took to the percussion instruments, which were introduced into European orchestras shortly afterward.

The percussion section in an orchestra is part of the rich art heritage from the Ottoman Empire. Europe also prized what they referred to as Turkey carpets. These carpets are still prized as elegant pieces of home and office furnishings in many places in the world. The empire's most lasting legacy, however, are the mosques designed by Süleyman's architect, Sinan, most of which are still standing.

Most historians view the Ottoman as the last of the ancient empires, but some also see it as the first Muslim-influenced government. This places the empire in a unique place in history. At the height of the empire, the Ottoman stood in the middle of the known civilized world and, through conquest and trade, allowed the cultures of the East and the West to meet and mingle. Begun by a nomadic tribal leader, the empire ended when the sultan was forced to step down in favor of a republic, a representative government elected by the people. The Ottoman Empire's six-hundred-year history places it as the government of transition between historic and modern times in the Middle East.

NOTES

Chapter 1: Islam Guided the Government

1. Quoted in Jason Goodwin, *Lords of the Horizons, A History of the Ottoman Empire.* New York: Henry Holt, 1998, p. 61.

Chapter 2: Families, Homes, and Clothing

2. Quoted in Goodwin, *Lords of the Horizons,* p. 149.
3. Quoted in Goodwin, *Lords of the Horizons,* p. 133.

Chapter 3: Work and Relaxation

4. Quoted in Goodwin, *Lords of the Horizons,* p. 196.

Chapter 4: Enduring Art and Architecture of the Ottomans

5. Quoted in Raphaela Lewis, *Everyday Life in Ottoman Turkey.* New York: Dorset, 1971, p. 153.

GLOSSARY

contemporary: Someone who is about the same age and lives during the same time period as another.

cuerda seca: Lost wax method of glazing ceramic tiles.

devshirme: The collecting of non-Muslim boys to serve as slaves to the sultan.

fetva: The answer to a legal question put before a mufti.

hane: A household that contained a married man with an independent income and his dependents.

harem: Living quarters for Muslim women to shelter them from the view of men who were not their relatives.

jinni: Magical mythical beings that were created out of fire, able to change shape or become invisible, enjoyed human pleasures, and lived long lives before dying.

muezzin: Mosque official who chants the call to prayer.

mufti: Member of the ulema appointed as legal adviser.

pilgrimage: A journey to a holy place.

qadi: Member of the ulema appointed as a judge.

republic: A representative government elected by the people.

sumptuary laws: Laws based on moral and/or religious grounds that banned extravagant spending.

ulema: Educated leaders of law and religion.

For More Information

Books

Luis A. Baralt, *Enchantment of the World: Turkey*. Danbury, CT: Childrens, 1997.

Raphaela Lewis, *Everyday Life in Ottoman Turkey*. New York: Dorset, 1977.

Websites

The Ottomans (www.wsu.edu). An Internet classroom anthology by Richard Hooker.

Index

Picture Credits

About the Author

Lucile Davis enjoys writing about history and geography. A full-time writer and author of nineteen books, she lives in Texas with her mother and brother.